Worship BAND PLAY-ALONG

He Is Exalted

Recorded and produced by Jim Reith at BeatHouse Music, Milwaukee, WI

Lead Vocals by Tonia Emrich and Jim Reith
Background Vocals by Jim Reith and Joy Palisoc Bach
Guitar by Jim Reith
Bass by Chris Kringel
Keyboard by Kurt Cowling
Drums by Del Bennett

ISBN 978-1-4234-1728-6

HAL•LEONARD® CORPORATION

7777 W. BLUEMOUND RD. P.O. BOX 13819 MILWAUKEE, WI 53213

Visit Hal Leonard Online at
www.halleonard.com

He Is Exalted

Beautiful One

Words and Music by Tim Hughes

Won - der - ful, so ___ won - der - ful is Your un - fail - ing ___ love. Your cross has spo - ken

God of All

Words and Music by Twila Paris

Moderately (= 89)

Intro

A **Verse**

God of all, __ we come to praise __ You. __ We lift Your name __ on high __ in all the earth. __

(We lift ___ Your name ___ on high, ___ we lift Your name ___ on high.) ___

God of all, ___

(We lift ___ Your name ___ on high, ___ we lift Your name ___ on high.) ___

God of all, ___

(We lift ___ Your name ___ on high, ___ we lift Your name ___ on high.) ___

God of all. ___

He Is Exalted

Words and Music by Twila Paris

Capo III

TRACKS
5/6

With a lilt (♩. = 57)

Intro

*Symbols in parentheses represent chord names respective to capoed guitar.
Symbols above reflect actual sounding chords. Capoed fret is "0" in tab.
Chord symbols represent overall harmony.

A **Verse**

He is ex-alt-ed, the King is ex-alt-ed on high; I will praise Him. He is ex-alt-ed, for-

In Christ Alone

Words and Music by Keith Getty
and Stuart Townend

With conviction (= 78)

Lord Most High

Words and Music by Don Harris and Gary Sadler

Lord, Reign in Me

Words and Music by Brenton Brown

We Want to See Jesus Lifted High

Words and Music by Doug Horley

C **Chorus 1**

We want to see, we want to see, we want to see Je-

-sus lift-ed high. ____ We want to see, we want to see,

Interlude

we want to see Je-sus lift-ed high. ____

Worthy Is the Lamb

Words and Music by Darlene Zschech

BEAUTIFUL ONE

TIM HUGHES

Key of **D Major**, 4/4

INTRO:

G   A   Bm7   A
G   A   D

VERSE 1:

G   A   D/F♯
Wonderful, so wonderful is Your unfailing love
        G   A   Bm7
Your cross has spoken mercy over me
      G   A   D/F♯
No eye has seen, no ear has heard, no heart could fully know
        G   A   D
How glorious, how beautiful You are

CHORUS:

          G   A   G   A
Beautiful One I love, Beautiful One I adore
          G   A   D
Beautiful One, my soul must sing

VERSE 2:

G   A   D/F♯
Powerful, so powerful, Your glory fills the skies
        G   A   Bm7
Your mighty works displayed for all to see
        G   A   D/F♯
The beauty of Your majesty awakes my heart to sing:
        G   A   D
How marvelous, how wonderful You are

(REPEAT CHORUS 2X)

BRIDGE (2X):

        G   A
You opened my eyes to Your wonders anew
        G   A
You captured my heart with this love
           G   A   D
'Cause nothing on earth is as beautiful as You

(REPEAT CHORUS 2X)

GOD OF ALL

TWILA PARIS

**TRACKS
3/4**

Key of **E Major**, 4/4

INTRO (2X):

E   B/D♯   C♯m7   Bsus

VERSE:

E   B/D♯
God of all, we come to praise You

   A/C♯   Bsus
We lift Your name on high in all the earth

E   B/D♯
God of all, we come to praise You

   A/C♯   Bsus
We lift Your name on high in all the earth

CHORUS 1:

       E/G♯ Bsus   B   E/G♯   Bsus   B
God of glo - ry,   God of maj - es - ty

       E/G♯ Bsus E/G♯   A   Bsus
God of mer - cy, we lift Your name on high

       E   A Bsus   E   A Bsus
God of all,   God of all

(REPEAT VERSE)

CHORUS 2:

       E/G♯   Bsus   B   E/G♯   Bsus   B
God of ho - li - ness,   God of righteousness

       E/G♯ Bsus E/G♯   A   Bsus
God of heav - en, we lift Your name on high

       E/G♯ Bsus   B   E/G♯   Bsus   B
God of glo - ry,   God of maj - es - ty

       E/G♯ Bsus E/G♯   A   Bsus
God of mer - cy, we lift Your name on high

TAG:

       E   A   Bsus
God of all (We lift Your name on high, we lift Your name on high) *REPEAT 4X*

       E (hold)
God of all

HE IS EXALTED

TWILA PARIS

 TRACKS
5/6

Key of **F Major**, 6/8

CAPO III (D MAJOR)

Chord symbols represent overall harmony for capoed guitar.
See page 16 for actual sounding chords.

INTRO:

D A/D G/D

D A/D G/D

VERSE:

D   D/F♯   G
He is exalted, the King is exalted on high

      G/B A/C♯
I will praise Him

D   D/F♯
He is exalted, forever exalted

  G A/G   G/A A Bsus B/A
And I   will   praise His name

CHORUS:

Em Bm/D   A/C♯ A
He   is the Lord

     D   F♯m7   G   D/F♯
Forever His truth shall reign

Em Bm/D   A/C♯ A
Heav - en and earth

     D   F♯m7 G   D/F♯
Rejoice in His holy name

Em Em/D   C   G/A   (D)
He is exalted, the King is exalted on high

(REPEAT INTRO)

(REPEAT VERSE)

(REPEAT CHORUS 2X)

TAG:

A/B B/D♯ Em Em/D   C   G/A   D (hold)
          He is exalted, the King is exalted on high

IN CHRIST ALONE

KEITH GETTY and STUART TOWNEND

Key of **D Major**, 3/4

INTRO (2X):

Am7   Em7   D Dsus D

VERSE 1:

  G/D   D   G   A
In Christ alone my hope is found

D/F♯   G   Em7 Asus   D
He is my light, my strength,   my song

   G/D   D   G   A
This Cornerstone, this solid ground

D/F♯   G   Em7 Asus   D
Firm through the fiercest drought and storm

    D/F♯   G   D/F♯   A
What heights of love, what depths of peace

    D/F♯   G   Bm7   A
When fears are stilled when strivings cease

   G   D   G   A
My Comforter, my All in All

D/F♯   G   Em7 Asus D
Here in the love of Christ   I stand

(Dsus D)

VERSE 2:

In Christ alone, who took on flesh
Fullness of God in helpless Babe
This gift of love and righteousness
Scorned by the ones He came to save
'Til on that cross as Jesus died
The wrath of God was satisfied
For ev'ry sin on Him was laid
Here in the death of Christ I live

INTERLUDE:

Am7   Em7   D Dsus D

VERSE 3:

There in the ground His body lay
Light of the world by darkness slain
Then bursting forth in glorious day
Up from the grave He rose again!
And as He stands in victory
Sin's curse has lost its grip on me
For I am His and He is mine
Bought with the precious blood of Christ

(Dsus D)

VERSE 4:

No guilt in life, no fear in death
This is the pow'r of Christ in me
From life's first cry to final breath
Jesus commands my destiny
No pow'r of hell, no scheme of man
Can ever pluck me from His hand
'Til He returns or calls me home
Here in the pow'r of Christ I'll stand

TAG:

    D/F♯   G   D/F♯   A
No pow'r of hell, no scheme of man

    D/F♯ G   Bm7   A
Can ever pluck me from His hand

   G   D   G   A
'Til He returns or calls me home

D/F♯   G   Em7 Asus   D
Here in the pow'r of Christ   I'll stand

D/F♯   G   Em7 Asus   D (hold)
Here in the pow'r of Christ   I'll stand

LORD MOST HIGH

DON HARRIS and GARY SADLER

Key of **E Major**, 6/8

INTRO (2X):

E   Esus   E   Esus2

VERSE:

           E   *Echo:* **Esus**   **E**
From the ends of the earth (from the ends of the earth)
        B   **Bsus**   **B**
From the depths of the sea (from the depths of the sea)
      C#m7
From the heights of the heavens (from the heights of the heavens)
    A **E/A** **A**
Your name be praised
        E   **Esus**   **E**
From the hearts of the weak (from the hearts of the weak)
       B   **Bsus**   **B**
From the shouts of the strong (from the shouts of the strong)
     C#m7
From the lips of all people (from the lips of all people)
    A **E/A** **A**   **B**
This song we raise, Lord

CHORUS 1:

E E/G#   A   B
Throughout the endless ages
E E/G#   A   B
You will be crowned with praises
C#m7 A Bsus B
Lord Most High
E   E/G#   A   B
Exalted in ev'ry nation
E   E/G#   A   B
Sov'reign of all creation
C#m7 A   B E/G#   A
Lord Most High, be magnified

(REPEAT VERSE)

CHORUS 2:

E E/G#   A   B
Throughout the endless ages
E E/G#   A   B
You will be crowned with praises
C#m7 A Bsus B
Lord Most High
E   E/G#   A   B
Exalted in ev'ry nation
E   E/G#   A   B
Sov'reign of all creation
C#m7 A Bsus B
Lord Most High

(REPEAT CHORUS 1)

TAG:

B   E E/G# A
    Be magnified   ***REPEAT 2X***
B   E (hold)
Be magnified

LORD, REIGN IN ME
BRENTON BROWN

Key of **G Major**, 4/4

INTRO:

G D C   G D C

VERSE 1:

G   D   C   D
   Over all the earth, You reign on high

G   D   C   D
   Ev'ry mountain stream, ev'ry sunset sky

Em7   D   C   D Am7
   But my one request, Lord, my only aim

         C   D
Is that You'd reign in me again

CHORUS:

G   D   C   D
   Lord, reign in me, reign in Your pow'r

G   D   C   D
   Over all my dreams, in my darkest hour

Em7   D   C   D Am7
   You are the Lord of all I am

         C   D
So won't You reign in me again?

INTERLUDE:

G D C   G D C

VERSE 2:

G   D   C   D
   Over ev'ry thought, over ev'ry word

G   D   C   D
   May my life reflect the beauty of my Lord

Em7   D   C   D Am7
   'Cause You mean more to me than any earthly thing

         C   D
So won't You reign in me again?

(REPEAT CHORUS 3X)

TAG:

Am7   C   D
   Won't You reign in me again?

OUTRO:

G D C   G D C (hold)

WE WANT TO SEE JESUS LIFTED HIGH

DOUG HORLEY

Key of **G Major**, 4/4

INTRO (2X):

G D   Em C

VERSE:

G   D
   We want to see Jesus lifted high

Em   C
   A banner that flies across this land

G   D
   That all men might see the truth and know

Em   C
   He is the way to heaven

(REPEAT VERSE)

CHORUS 1:

G   D
   We want to see,   we want to see

Em   C   G/B Am7   G
   We want to see Je - sus   lift - ed high

G   D
   We want to see,   we want to see

Em   C   G/B Am7   G
   We want to see Je - sus   lift - ed high

INTERLUDE:

G D   Em C

(REPEAT VERSE & CHORUS 1)

BRIDGE:

              D   Em
Step by step, we're moving forward

            D   Em
Little by little, taking ground

             D   Em
Ev'ry prayer a pow'rful weapon

                C   D
Strongholds come tumbling down
   and down and down and down

(REPEAT VERSE & CHORUS 1)

CHORUS 2:

G   D
   We're gonna see,   we're gonna see

Em   C   G/B Am7   G
   We're gonna see Je - sus   lift - ed high

G   D
   We're gonna see,   we're gonna see

Em   C   G/B Am7   G
   We're gonna see Je - sus   lift - ed high

OUTRO: *(Vocal ad lib.)*

G D   Em C

G D   Em C G/B Am7 G

WORTHY IS THE LAMB

DARLENE ZSCHECH

Key of **G Major**, 4/4

INTRO:

Em7   G   Em7   G

VERSE:

                    C   G/B
Thank You for the cross, Lord

                    C   D   G
Thank You for the price You paid

                D/E   Em7   D   C
Bearing all my sin and shame, in love You came

   Am7   G/B   D
And gave amazing grace

G   G/B   C   G/B
Thank You for this love, Lord

                   C   D   G
Thank You for the nail-pierced hands

                D/E   Em7   D   C
Washed me in Your cleansing flow, now all I know:

     Am7   G/B   D
Your forgiveness and embrace

CHORUS:

G   D/F♯ Am7 G/B   C
Worthy is the Lamb, seated on the throne

D   D/C   G/B   C   Am7   C/G   D   D/F♯
Crown You now with many crowns, You reign victorious

G   D/F♯ Am7 G/B   C
High and lifted up,   Jesus, Son of God

    D   D/C   G/B C   Dsus
The Treasure of heaven crucified

       Am7   G/B   C
Worthy is the Lamb

       Am7   G/B Dsus
Worthy is the Lamb

(REPEAT VERSE)

(REPEAT CHORUS 2X)

TAG:

                   Am7 G/B C
Worthy is the Lamb

                   Am7 G/B Dsus
Worthy is the Lamb

                   G (hold)
Worthy is the Lamb